IT WAS HIM, Not Me

HOW TO RECLAIM YOUR POWER AND LEARN TO LIVE BEYOND CHILDHOOD SEXUAL TRAUMA

MONIQUE PETERKIN

Monique Peterkin. © 2020

All rights reserved. No part of this book may be reproduced, stored, or transmitted by any means- whether auditory, graphic, mechanical, or electronic- without written permission of both publisher and author, except in the case of brief excerpts used in critical articles and certain other noncommercial uses permitted by copyright law. Unauthorized reproduction of any part of this work is illegal and is punishable by law.

ISBN: 978-0-578-81614-2

Because of the dynamic nature of the internet, any web addresses or links contained in this book may have changed since publication and may no longer be valid. The views expressed in this work are solely those of the author and do not necessarily reflect the views of the publisher, and the publisher disclaims any responsibility for them.

Printed in the United States of America
https://www.moniquepeterkin.com

Contents

Dedication v
Introduction vii

1. A Victim of Childhood Sexual Trauma 1
2. Accessibility 6
3. Reclaiming my voice 15
4. The Lies And Truths Of Sexual Trauma 20
5. The "Why" Does Not Matter 38
6. Restoring Trust In Myself 41
7. Learning to Live Beyond My Sexual Trauma 48
8. Accepting My Abuser Was Free and Wouldn't Face Justice 52
9. Living In My Window 56
10. My Nights Were Not My Own; They Were For My Demons 65
11. This Is My Story I Will Use My Voice 71
12. This Is My Body, And I Am In Charge 76
13. The Manipulated Becomes the Manipulator 80
14. Taking back my happiness 84

Conclusion 91
About the Author 101

Dedication

I would like to thank my mother,

Nathalee Williams, for always standing in front, behind, and by my side through my journey to reclaim my power and find my voice to speak up against sexual violence. My sister, Nevaeh Williams, for teaching me how to love without limit, and my dad Norris Williams, for showing me what a healthy relationship with a male should be.

Sexual trauma is an experience that no one should have to endure in their life. The psychological and physical toll it takes on one's mind, body, and soul is indescribable. I know first hand what this feels like as I have too struggled with the psychological consequences of childhood sexual trauma.

This book is dedicated to the survivors whose voices have been silenced by fear, guilt, and or shame; I want you to know I hear you, I believe you, I feel your pain, and you are stronger than you think.

Introduction

Welcome to my book, *Reclaiming Your Life After Childhood Sexual Trauma*. You have set the wheels in motion for your journey to heal and live beyond your trauma. I hope that as you delve into this book, you will come to realize that you are a victor and no longer the victim. You will learn how implementing simple techniques and completing the worksheets provided in this book. You can combat the negative emotional responses most women feel after surviving childhood sexual trauma.

This book addresses how to identify your emotional and physical triggers by using The Window of Tolerance, which is a simple tool to understand and carry out emotional regulation to minimize negative and unwanted emotions. If you are reading this book, chances are your abuser is still walking free and you are reminded of what they did to you without facing judgment. By the end of this book, you will know how to take back the power that was stolen from you and live beyond your sexual traumatic experiences

The strategies and processes that I have included in this book have changed my narrative and mindset regarding my sexual traumatic experiences. I will share how I learned to recognize the signs of oncoming anxiety attacks and intercept them, control my erratic breathing, and rid myself of nightmares and insomnia.

The hardest thing I had to face in my journey was accepting that I was a victim of childhood sexual trauma. It solidified what my mind tried to protect me from. It made it real but the acknowledgment and acceptance of what I endured was a gateway that sped up the process of my healing journey. In my journey, I had to embrace my feelings and emotions. I had to validate how I felt; the anger, the pain, the confusion, the hurt. Spending so many years blaming myself and disregarding my feelings surrounding my sexual trauma. I found it difficult not to judge how negative I felt towards myself. I found it hard not to blame myself for being raped. I felt I was not justified in being angry, hurt, and confused because I brought my sexual trauma onto myself. In the end, I found clarity and inner strength. I was able to see beyond my pain and suffering, which allowed me to heal without judgment.

CHAPTER 1
▼

A Victim of Childhood Sexual Trauma

Sexual abuse is described as unwanted sexual activities with the perpetrators who use force, make threats, or take advantage of victims who are not able to give their consent. Most victims and perpetrators know each other. Immediate reactions following sexual abuse range from shock, fear, and/or disbelief. In 2020, I conducted a study for a course I took at Northcentral University that revealed that one out of four girls and one out of six boys surveyed experienced childhood sexual abuse before the age of 18.

At the age of seven, my sexual trauma began. My abuser, whom I will call Damien for the remainder of this book, orchestrated a situation I did not comprehend and started manipulating and grooming me to fit his needs. It began with small touches, such as rubbing his hands up and down my arms and playing with my hair, buying me candies, or bringing presents for me but not the other children. Damien made me feel like I was his special friend. When no one was looking he would pepper me with kisses on my face and neck and tickle me, this brought my guards down and I became used to his presence and touches when no one was around.

You may be wondering where my parents were while this was happening. My dad did not live with us and my mom had to work in the United States to provide money for me to go to school and have necessities. I was left in the care of my aunt, who had her own child who was younger than me. She also had to work and back in those days leaving a child at home alone was common in Jamaica.

I did not understand how my abuser was always there when I was alone. Whether it was playing in the backyard by myself or walking home from school. He always gave me his undivided attention and always wanted to be in physical contact with me either by holding my hand or giving me piggyback rides. I started believing that the attention I got was because I was his only friend. I did not expect that this would turn into something darker and more sinister as time progressed.

The first time that the rape took place, I was at home by myself and my aunt had gone to work. I remember I was washing the dishes and heard the back door open. When I went to see who it was, I found Damien standing there. He asked if I was alone and I said yes. He advanced toward me. This was not like the other times where he found me alone, I recall feeling afraid like I was backed into a corner by a big dog. I was scared, anxious, and in complete disbelief that this person I trusted suddenly made me feel unsafe. When he got to me, he told me we were going to play a game. I did not understand why he wanted me to take off his clothes. I did not know why he was showing me his private parts. I tried to cover my eyes, but he told me I had to watch him. It was a complete shock to me, and I was too fearful that if I did not do what he said, he would be angry with me and hurt me. After he was done taking off his clothes he proceeded to take mine off, I was no match for him and my attempt at telling him no and stopping him from taking my clothes off was unsuccessful. He eventually got my clothes off and then sexually abused me. The aftermath of this traumatic event left me feeling confused and numb. At the age of seven I was unable to verbally describe my feelings and emotions after the rape happened. I did not understand why Damien did what he did.

After moving from my childhood home in Jamaica at the age of 12 to live with my mother in another parish, I finally understood that the friendship with Damien was not a friendship at all. Instead, it was a manipulated situation in which I was the victim and he was my abuser. I came to this realization in the sixth grade. During biology class, the teacher was teaching us about the male and female reproductive organs. She taught us the difference between sexual intercourse between two consenting adults over 18 and rape. I learned that what I went through was not only illegal, but it was not healthy, and none of my friends were experiencing these types of sexual acts.

I was unaware of being sexually groomed to fit the needs of my perpetrator. I thought that other little girls my age were going through the same experiences because he told me that all of the girls my age had to do it and that it is a rite of passage to be a grown-up. He said the only way we could be friends was by letting him have sex with me. I had known Damien all my life and he was a friend of the family who lived in the same neighborhood. I thought that it was okay to be his friend as well. I wanted to be a grown-up too, which meant I had to endure what was being done to me. I had to be compliant and allow this person to use my body and gain pleasure from it.

Children are unable to tell the difference between what is inappropriate behavior and what is not. A predator crossing these lines will know how to manipulate their victims into thinking they have no choice in the matter but to endure the demands of the predator. If I were still at the age that my abuse happened, I would have liked for someone to explain to me the different body parts, what is considered inappropriate and appropriate behavior, and that it is okay to tell someone when another person is being inappropriate towards me. I wish someone told me that it is my body, and I am in charge of it—not someone else.

CHAPTER 2

Accessibility

I spent 8 years confronting my inner child, trying to go through therapy, or trying to understand. Why me? Why was I chosen? Why was I victimized? Why did I have to develop mental illness as a result, because some asshole decided that I was the perfect victim for him? I never got answers to these questions. I felt cheated. I felt that someone was to be held responsible, and I lashed out at my therapist and anyone that I could lash out at because no one ever gave me a straight answer as to why I was targeted.

During my healing journey, I came to realize that it is all about accessibility for the abusers. There's nothing in particular about me or anyone else who is targeted as a child. I did not pursue this form of interaction with anyone. Instead, I was a child who was accessible. That is the only answer I have concluded as the reason for being chosen. I was easily accessible and easily manipulated.

During the time with Damien, I did not know an adult and child should not have a "friendship" like what we had. I did not understand why I should not have been having such a friendship with an adult. I did not know why we always had to play when no one else was around or why I could not tell anyone what we were doing.

On my journey, I learned that people who do not have control over their lives tend to take their frustrations out on those who are more vulnerable than they are. In this sense, when someone feels like their life is out of control, they will do everything in their power to regain some form of control. They prey on the vulnerability of a person. When someone is vulnerable, predators find it less complicated to take advantage of their target. Predators thrive on having emotional and physical control over someone. They find pleasure in dominating others, and children become targeted because they are unable to protect themselves and are most often easily controlled.

The power dynamic is a desirable one, and one that is attainable when it involves children. I was a quiet child who always wanted to play with everyone around me, including my abuser. I was the older cousin who looked after everyone around me and made sure that everyone had lunch and did their chores because I was a people-pleaser. I felt the need to please those around me to show that I was a good child.

During my abuse, I felt that if I pleased Damien, I would not get in trouble. Therefore, I would not be considered a "bad child," and the friendship would continue. In my mind, I would have a grown-up as a friend who looked after me and was always there when I was alone. I did not look at it from an adult's perspective. Simply put, an adult should not be touching, kissing, or penetrating a child. That is in no way a form of friendship. I was not aware that such a friendship was not only disturbing, but it put me in a position where I started isolating myself from my family and my younger cousins because Damien told me that I did not need those types of friendships. He told me that the only company I needed was him, and that's all that mattered. My emotional and physical state were under attack, and I did nothing to stop it. I didn't know how to stop it.

When I learned that most predators go for people who are easily accessible, I limited others' access to my physical and mental being. At the age of twenty-seven I made a pact with myself to no longer be the girl who allowed people to have full control of me, my time and body were my own. I control how much access a person has to me and how their action impacts me. I stopped surrounding myself with controlling individuals who demanded 100 percent of my time. I limited how available I was and set boundaries. I now maintain how and when I am open to people, both physically and mentally. Taking back control of my accessibility made me feel more in control of myself than ever. It was a feeling I began to crave. My mental health began to improve because my boundaries were clear and I did not feel obligated to anyone. What I gave to people was on my terms. I had more time to safeguard my emotional and physical wellbeing once I started limiting my accessibility. It has proven to be one of the most successful ways of taking back control.

Setting personal boundaries allowed me to set limits and rules for myself within all my relationships. By creating a healthy set of boundaries I was able to say "no" without fear or guilt. I was able to communicate more comfortably with those around me, knowing I had set boundaries. The feeling of obligation was no longer present when I was uncomfortable with doing something because I learned how to say no.

At the end of this chapter, you will learn how you too can create your personal boundaries by utilizing the Personal Boundaries Worksheet.

Setting Personal Boundaries

Personal boundaries can be classified as the limitations and rules one sets for themselves within relationships. An individual who has healthy boundaries in place has the ability to say "no" to others when and if they deem fit, but they are comfortable and capable of opening up themselves to intimacy and other forms of a relationship without feeling fear or guilt.

FIGURE OUT YOUR BOUNDARIES

Setting boundaries should reflect your values or things that you consider to be important. An example would be, if you spend quality time with family, or create a set time frame for working late

The boundaries you set are yours, and yours alone. Some of your boundaries might be in alignment with those close to you, but others can be one of a kind.

Before entering a situation be clear on your boundaries. This in turn will make it easier to determine what you are comfortable doing.

WHAT YOU CAN SAY

It is your right to say "no". When saying "no" be sure to express yourself clearly and without uncertainty so there is no doubt about what you want and are comfortable with.

"I do not feel comfortable with this"   "This does not work for me"

"I am asking you please do not do that"   "This is unacceptable"

"I have decided not to"   I do not want to do that"

WHAT YOU CAN DO

- **Be confident** in your body language. Maintain eye contact, maintain a steady tone of voice at an acceptable volume (not too low, and not too high)

- **Be respectful**, steer clear of yelling, shaming, or being rude. You can be firm in your stance, but maintain a respectful tone as this will enable your message to be better received.

- **Plan for the ahead,** when faced with a difficult situation, thinking ahead about what you want to say can help you feel more confident in your answer and position.

- **Know when to compromise**, it is always helpful when you listen and take into consideration the other person's point of view. Note: You never have to compromise if you do not wish to do so, but give & take, is important to any healthy relationship

Setting Personal Boundaries

Instructions: In this exercise respond to the following questions as though they were real life scenarios.

EXAMPLES:

SITUATION: You are sharing an apartment/house with a roommate, he/she has been partaking in your food. However, both you and your roommate have never set specific boundaries regarding sharing personal items such as your food. You find this to be a problem and do not want him/she eating your food.

RESPONSE: "I would like to separate our foods. If there is something of mine you want specifically, please ask me before you take it."

SITUATION: You are in the middle of sleeping, and your friend calls at 11 pm to discuss issues he/she is having with their partner. You need to be awake by 5 am.

RESPONSE: "I understand that this situation is very upsetting to you. I would love to listen and talk to you regarding this, but I need to go to sleep. Can we catch up tomorrow afternoon when I am able to give you my full attention?"

PRACTICE:

SITUATION: You are in the middle of eating dinner when you hear the doorbell ring. There is a salesperson who is trying to sell you something. You are not interested and you try to politely turn them down, they keep on pitching their sale. You want to return to your meal.

RESPONSE:

Setting Personal Boundaries

PRACTICE:

SITUATION: You have invited company over for the evening, however, it is getting late and they show no signs of leaving any time soon. You need to prepare for bed, but your company does not seem to be aware of how late it is getting.

RESPONSE:

SITUATION: You have been invited out on a date with someone you consider to be a good friend. You have no interest in being more than platonic friends with this person. You would like to be clear and concise about your feelings towards them.

RESPONSE:

SITUATION: Your sister asks you to watch your niece and nephew over the weekend. You already made plans.

RESPONSE:

Reflection Questions:

1. At what age did I realize that my sexual trauma was rape and not my fault?
2. Do I feel obligated to please everyone around me even if it makes me uncomfortable?
3. How accessible am I to those around me?
4. Have I set healthy personal boundaries for myself?
5. Am I able to say NO when I feel uncomfortable about something?

CHAPTER 3

Reclaiming my voice

After sexual abuse has taken place, most children automatically believe that they are to be blamed. A child who has experienced pleasures during the abuse feels an even more significant burden of guilt. In my case, feeling like I was the reason why I was sexually abused was constant in my mind. I felt that I deserved what was happening because I did not speak up against it nor did I say no.

The longer my abuse happened, the more my reactions began to change with each experience. Gone were shock and disbelief. In their place were anxiety, guilt, and pleasure.

I felt dirty for feeling sexual pleasure during my abuse, and I often wonder if that is why I let it continue for so many years. I ask myself now as I did then, did I ask for it? Did I intentionally isolate myself so Damien would have the opportunity to rape me? Did I initiate it by being compliant? Did I seek him out? These questions increased my despair and made it hard initially to change the narrative from victim-blaming to being a childhood sexual abuse survivor.

I kept silent, and I paid for it with my body. Shame, guilt, and fear were the driving forces behind my silence for six years of my life. I will never gain those six years back, because I doubted the ability of people around me to believe and protect me during my abuse. I felt as though no one would look at me and see me as the victim; they would see me as the initiator. They would say I was asking for it like I've been told repeatedly by Damien. Because I kept silent, I believed I too was to be blamed for my sexual abuse therefore no one was going to believe that I was innocent if I myself did not believe it. People would see me as a troublemaker for disrupting the peace in my neighborhood by speaking out against the abuse. They would deem me a liar and a bad child.

Facing my abuser and confronting him publicly for what he did to me was not an experience I wanted to add to the list of traumatic experiences. I learned that I stayed in that situation out of fear of being publicly humiliated and condemned by family and friends.

The guilt and humiliation that come from being sexually abused are feelings that unless addressed, will forever plague you. In my case, I felt that I needed to be condemned because I allowed this predator, this pedophile, to use my body, influence how I looked at my family and how I lived life. I needed to be condemned because I was not strong enough to say no. I needed to be condemned because I found pleasure during my years of being raped. The guilt associated with sexual trauma is very common in survivors. Breaking away from that guilt not only took time but it also took patience, it took a lot of self-reassurance and validation on my part.

I remember one day prior to moving from my childhood home where my sexual trauma took place, I was at my aunt and uncle's house, and they had a party. I tried to be as invisible as I possibly could by staying out of the way of the adults, isolating myself, and not drawing attention to myself. Damien was in attendance and still somehow sought me out. He violated me two doors down from where everyone was partying. My thoughts were filled with being found out and being blamed, so I kept quiet and endured the onslaught. By doing this, it solidified for me that I was never going to get the help that I needed to get out of this situation.

I did not know at the time that someone would advocate on my behalf and say this is not right and advocate for Damien to face judgment for what he was doing to me. I didn't believe that anyone of that nature existed. I did not trust anyone to protect me and ensure my safety from this monster. I felt trapped; I felt as though my life would never be better unless I committed suicide to get myself out of the constant sexual abuse. I learned the hard way that being silent prolonged my sexual abuse; my silence afforded Damien the ability to carry out abusing me without facing judgment and without facing convention. My silence was an undeserving gift to Damien—a gift he willingly took from me and continued to use to reach his satisfaction.

As an adult, I have learned how to speak up for myself when I do not agree with something. No one will benefit from my silence any longer. Speaking up for myself means that I am no longer voiceless. My voice will be heard, I have something to say and I am saying it. It does not matter if it is family, friends, my doctors, or strangers. If something does not feel right or their actions are affecting me in some form, I let them know respectfully. I no longer feel the need to just sit back and take whatever is happening to me anymore in fear of repercussions. Whoever wants to be mad at me, so be it, but I am not going to be that silent girl any longer. My opinion matters, how I feel matters, decisions that affect me directly or indirectly matter. I no longer allow a person to rob me of my voice.

The power that comes from reclaiming my voice is wonderful. I feel stronger and more assured of myself. I speak up for myself as well as others and I feel bold and in control. This feeling has made my healing journey smoother as I no longer feel the burden by keeping my silence. I feel empowered and I love every minute of it.

Reflection Questions:

1. Am I to be blamed for my sexual trauma?
2. How has my silence about my rape affected my relationships?
3. Do I feel guilty for being sexually abused?
4. What are the words I use to describe myself after my sexual trauma?
5. Am I fearful of what others might think if I break my silence and tell them about my rape?

CHAPTER 4

The Lies And Truths Of Sexual Trauma

"You've been asking for this, always giving me those puppy dog eyes and that little smile." These are words Damien said to me. When I was eight years old, Damien started justifying why he was sexually abusing me. He told me I was asking for it, and I began believing him. I began thinking that all my small actions; smiling, breathing– even just merely existing, was asking for him to violate me.

At the age of 16, I moved to America with my mom and my stepdad. I thought that because I was no longer in the country in which my abuse happened that I was free of the trauma both physically and mentally. However, mentally I had spent 8 years of my childhood creating the story in my mind that my years as a sex abuse victim was because I asked for it. I must have initiated or invited Damien somehow. Accepting that my sexual abuse was not my fault was a hard pill to swallow, it was easier to blame myself than to blame him. I often found myself saying things such as "the rape was my fault, I should feel ashamed for letting him rape me, I am tainted and I do not deserve to be loved." I found comfort in blaming myself for my abuse because I truly believed I should have protected myself from Damien.

At some point in my life after leaving Jamaica and moving to America, my mind started repressing the events surrounding my sexual trauma. September 2010, at the age of 19, I enlisted in the United States Navy and began my military career. I was stationed in Atsugi, Japan. It was not until the age of 21, around March 2012, that memories of the abuse came flooding back, and I began experiencing flashbacks and fractured images of my abuser. In November 2012, I began experiencing extreme mood swings, constant nightmares that left me completely drenched in cold sweat many nights which led to me becoming severely depressed. The only way to combat these feelings and emotions was to get drunk to the point I felt nothing but numbness. I started taking over the counter nighttime cold medicine that would put me to sleep and keep me asleep. When my symptoms and behavior became noticeable to my shipmates and commander, I was mandated to see a psychiatrist to "sort myself out."

During my visit with the psychiatrist, I was medically diagnosed with bipolar one disorder, a mental disorder that causes an individual to experience extreme mood swings. The mood swings include extreme highs (mania)- having high amounts of energy which most often results in restlessness, euphoria (extreme happiness), not being able to sleep for long periods of time and difficulty keeping focused, indulging in behaviors others might deem risky such as speeding, and in my case hypersexuality.In some cases extreme lows (depression). I was also diagnosed with severe PTSD and anxiety disorder. For two years I was heavily medicated which left me numb to the world. I found no joy in the world around me and just became indifferent to everyone. The colors of the world became dull. They lost their vibrancy and excitement. I hated every minute of being on those medications.

In September 2014, I was medically discharged from the military, I continued therapy outside of active duty and began trying to wean off the heavy doses of medication. I did not just want to numb the feelings and emotions, I wanted to understand them and figure out a way to heal myself while being lucid. During my years of therapy, I discovered that having sex and doing sexual acts that I did not want to do was the way I believed I would be loved and accepted because Damien told me he supposedly loved me whenever he was done raping me. I started associating love with sex and it carried on into my adult life. I wouldn't tell my family and friends that I love them because they weren't having sex with me therefore they did not love me. Physically, I had no outward trauma of my abuse, but mentally I was in a fight for my very life because what is considered normal wasn't consistent with my normal. I felt isolated, depressed, dirty, and disgusted on a consistent basis when I remembered that at some point throughout the years of being raped, I felt pleasure from my abuse. I became more ashamed and blamed myself even more for what I suffered. My body reacted involuntarily to what had been done to it. I later learned that experiencing sexual pleasure from my abuse was not uncommon. At one point in time, I believed that I was a dirty whore, for feeling pleasure derived from my abuse and I struggled with believing that I actually wanted Damien to rape me because physically, it felt good. . I recall instances during the years of sexual abuse, I became accustomed to the intrusions of my abuser. Instead of being scared, I felt guilty that I was gaining some form of gratification from being repeatedly raped. I became accustomed to the pretty words Damien used to coax me into submission and a more relaxed frame of mind. I did not know how to decipher my emotions. After much therapy, I later learned that the actions caused feelings in me that were described as anxiety from knowing he would eventually find me alone again, pleasure from what he did when he did find me alone, and guilt for feeling pleasure from my rape.

Unbeknownst to me, I started creating unhealthy sexual habits to gain better control of my emotions and to prove that I liked whatever was considered regular sex. I felt that to rid myself of these dirty, unwanted images that consistently plagued me, I needed to replace them with newer, more pleasurable moments that I consented to. I needed to be in control of sexual gratification during intercourse. In doing so, I believed I would destroy the guilt I felt for being a victim and for experiencing pleasure during those horrendous acts.

During the time period of my abuse, I would sometimes experience arousal when the abuse was taking place, the feeling of guilt I experienced because of my arousal during the act was not me enjoying what was being done to me but my body's reaction. I learned through therapy that being raped and experiencing arousal can happen simultaneously, and one does not always exclude the other.. That is not to say that what I experienced is any less traumatic or any less non-consensual. Take, for instance, being tickled . Even though this action can be considered pleasurable and can make you laugh, it is most often done against your wishes. Tickling can also be very unpleasant to some individuals, and even though that individual is asking the tickler to stop, they continue laughing because they cannot help reacting to the sensation, which encourages the tickler to continue because as far as they know you are enjoying it.

In August 2018, after battling with these feelings of isolation from family and friends and disgust because I experienced pleasure during my rape, I felt that I did not deserve to be alive and be happy. I felt dirty and damaged beyond repair and suicide was the only way to end these feelings. My mind got to a place where I truly believed the only way out was to die. This led me to a mental facility where I was put on psychiatric hold for two weeks. In these two weeks, I had no privacy and a nurse was no more than 3-4 feet away from me at all times; while I slept, showered, used the restroom, and ate. It was at this time that I realized that I had hit rock bottom and couldn't climb my way out without professional help, I also realized that there were people who cared about my life and loved me genuinely. Did it take away my history of sexual abuse? No, but it made me see that my life mattered and that it's okay to ask for professional help when doing it on your own is just not cutting it. It also prompted me to find healthy and realistic ways to manage the psychological consequences of being raped as a child. I began to seek additional ways to reclaim the power of my mind and soul and lived beyond my sexual trauma beside medication and therapy.

I learned through therapy that blaming myself for other people's actions towards me did nothing but stress me out, give me anxiety, lead me into a major depression, and cause me to lose trust in every single person whom I came across. But I did not know how to change my mindset. In order to heal I had to undo the way I thought. The first thing I did was figure out a way to get my thoughts and feelings out of my head and heart. I began journaling and recording my emotions. I wrote in capital letters and shouted, screamed, and cursed while I recorded. I did not limit myself to my choices of words either. I was mad and angry and I needed to express exactly how I was feeling. Afterward, I felt purged of my ugly thoughts and I deleted the recording and ripped up the journal pages as a way of cleansing my mind and heart. I made a habit of doing this daily. After a couple of months, I started to see a change in the direction of my thoughts, feelings, and emotions. I still felt angry and mad about what happened to me but then I started blaming myself less. I cursed and shouted less. I truly began accepting that I was not in a position to defend myself and I shifted from victim-blaming to blaming my abuser. I began to validate feelings and not judge or feel ashamed of how I felt. This became my self-therapy where I did not have to pretend I had it all together or that I was completely healed from my trauma. I allowed myself to drop my guard and be genuine with myself.

After a year of journaling and recording, I began to breathe easier. I interacted with people more and allowed myself to open up about what I went through without going into a rage and lashing out. I became outspoken against sexual abuse and became an advocate by telling my story to those willing to listen. I felt I was reclaiming my power each time I told my story, I felt like a survivor, a victor who went to hell and back and lived to tell the tale.

During one of my journaling sessions, I found myself writing the lies I have been blaming myself for. I noticed that not once did I blame Damien for what he did. I needed to change this narrative in order to proceed with my healing journey, for each time I blamed myself, I asked out loud "why do you believe?" I would then write the reason why I believed I was to be blamed. I would then write the reason why a child who has been sexually assaulted should not be blamed for what he/she went through. What I noticed was that I never blamed a child for what their abuser did to them, but with myself, I was placing the blame on me, instead of on Damien.

To better understand the exercise I have compiled a shortlist of lies, the reason why I believe the lies and actual truth statements that helped me change my thought process of blaming myself for my sexual trauma.

Lie:
I am the reason my abuse happened.

The reason why: If I had spoken up when Damien first raped me, he would not have repeatedly raped me. He raped me because I did not say no to him. I deserve him raping me because why else would I have found pleasure when he continued raping me for years.

Truth:
The sexual trauma I experienced was not my fault:

The reason why: My sexual trauma was not my fault because I was a child and I did not ask to be raped or taken advantage of. No one deserved to be taken advantage of or raped. The fault was not mine but my rapist. I was a vulnerable and accessible child that he saw the opportunity to take advantage of.

Lie:
I should be ashamed of myself because of the abuse I experienced.

I am a disgrace to my family, I let a grown man see my naked 7-year-old body, I am a disgusting human being. No one is going to love me because I am tainted and dirty.

Truth:
There is no reason I should feel ashamed for experienced sexual trauma.

This is my body, and I love my body, it is not dirty or tainted. I was a victim of sexual assault, I will not let my abuser win. Rape is not who I am, is it was something I experienced. I am beautiful, I am kind, I am worthy of all good things.

Located at the end of this chapter is a guided Truth & Lies activity sheet that can help you separate the lies and truth surrounding your sexual trauma.

Lies & Truths Example Activity Sheet

In order to rewire the brain with permanent truths, we need to speak the truths about sexual trauma and align our thoughts with those truths. By reprogramming the lies we tell ourselves with the truths about sexual trauma.

Lie: I am the reason my abuse happened.

••

The reason why: If I had spoken up when Damien first raped me, he would not have repeatedly raped me. He raped me because I did not say no to him. I deserve him raping me because why else would I have found pleasure when he continued raping me for years.

••

Truth: The sexual trauma I experienced was not my fault:

••

The reason why: My sexual trauma was not my fault because I was a child and I did not ask to be raped or taken advantage of. No one deserved to be taken advantage of or raped. The fault was not mine but my rapist. I was a vulnerable and accessible child that he saw the opportunity to take advantage of.

••

IT WAS HIM, NOT ME

Lie Activity Sheet
Describe how the six lies about sexual trauma present themselves in your life

I am the cause of my abuse.

....
....
....
....
....
....

I should feel ashamed of my sexual abuse

....
....
....
....
....
....

Lie Activity Sheet

Describe how the six lies about sexual trauma present themselves in your life

I am not good enough.

....
....
....
....
....
....

I have no power in my life

....
....
....
....
....
....

Lie Activity Sheet

Describe how the six lies about sexual trauma present themselves in your life

I do not deserve to be happy.

....
....
....
....
....
....

I am not worthy of being loved.

....
....
....
....
....
....

Truth Activity Sheet

To rewire the brain with permanent truths, we need to speak the truths about sexual trauma and align our thoughts with those truths. By reprogramming the lies, we tell ourselves the truths about sexual trauma.

Write down why these truths listed are true about your sexual trauma.

My worth is not dependent on my sexual trauma.

....
....
....
....
....

I am not ashamed aboubt my sexual trauma.

....
....
....
....
....
....

Truth Activity Sheet

To rewire the brain with permanent truths, we need to speak the truths about sexual trauma and align our thoughts with those truths. By reprogramming the lies, we tell ourselves the truths about sexual trauma.

Write down why these truths listed are true about your sexual trauma.

I am not to be blamed for my sexual trauma.

....
....
....
....
....
....

I am a powerful individudal.

....
....
....
....
....
....

Truth Activity Sheet

To rewire the brain with permanent truths, we need to speak the truths about sexual trauma and align our thoughts with those truths. By reprogramming the lies, we tell ourselves the truths about sexual trauma.

Write down why these truths listed are true about your sexual trauma.

I deserve to be happy.

....
....
....
....
....
....

I am a good person.

....
....
....
....
....
....

Reflection Questions:

1. Do I believe I am at fault for my rape?
2. How does past sexual abuse currently affect intimacy with my partner?
3. Have I created unhealthy sexual habits because of my past trauma?
4. How has my rape affected me mentally?
5. What are some of the ways that I cope with my past trauma?

CHAPTER 5

The "Why" Does Not Matter

After spending a year writing and recording my feelings, I thought I was truly healed. I felt I did not need therapy or medication anymore, but that was far from the truth. I still constantly found myself asking "why me, why did he have to choose me?" I wanted to know the reasons behind why I was targeted, why he chose to rape a child. I did not have the answers to these questions and they bothered me a great deal. I was trying to understand why Damien felt the need to take my innocence and abuse me for years.

I learned that focusing on the specific events of my abuse and the motives of my abuser was part of why I could not heal. I felt that if I knew every detail of his motives for targeting me, I would be able to better understand why I became a victim. I realized that no matter how hard I tried to find answers, focusing on the abusive events and the motivations of my abuser will not give me the peace of mind I seek nor will it justify why I was targeted.

I stopped dwelling on the why's and the motivates surrounding my abuse. I had moved on and accepted that I was a victim of rape and I cannot turn back the hands of time. Acceptance is one of the hardest things to accomplish because it means the world isn't made up of all good people, there are bad people whose intention is to cause harm to those around them whether their victims are children or adults. This does not mean that I am desensitized to the horrors that bad people inflict. It just means I have accepted that I was a victim of circumstances. The circumstance of accessibility and caretakers who trusted Damien and never believed that he could rape me were out of my control. In order to continue my healing journey, I needed to stop dwelling on the motives that led to being abused.

Reflection Questions:

1. Am I ready to accept that I am not at fault for my rape?
2. Am I ready to accept that I am worthy of love and all good things in life?
3. How can I find peace with knowing that I was the victim of rape?
4. Have I truly healed from my past trauma?
5. Am I ready to take back my life?

CHAPTER 6

Restoring Trust In Myself

Abusers do not want you to trust your feelings. In most cases, when abuse happens, they tell you, if not explicitly then implicitly, that what you are feeling doesn't matter and those feelings are invalid.

I remember my sixth-grade teacher talking about sexual education and what a woman and a man do in order to have a baby. I knew right then and there that the sexual abuse I experienced at the hands of Damien was wrong on all levels because I was not a woman and I was not ready to have a baby. I did not know whom to trust with what was going on in my life. I did not trust my feelings and thoughts. Perhaps I was making it a bigger deal than it actually was. I thought I was overexaggerating. I was taught that my feelings were not to be trusted because what I was feeling was so at odds with what I was told. While I was feeling anxiety, guilt, remorse, and pleasure, my perpetrator expressed happy feelings, contentment, an extreme amount of pleasure, and no guilt or fear.

I learned that what took place was wrong but in my mind, I had no way out. I disregarded my feelings because my abuser told me that they did not matter. In fact, he made the statement, "you do not know what you want, so I'm giving you what you need." And I thought, *well, he's a grown-up, so he must know exactly what I need, and therefore he is doing this because he's a responsible adult, and what is being done to me is what responsible adults do.* It took me 22 years to trust my feelings and instincts. In doing so, I was embracing what I was feeling on an emotional and physical level. I now use my instincts and my feelings to determine what situations suit me best, what situations are good for me emotionally and mentally, and what situations are not. I use my feelings and emotions to dictate how I live my life.

I learned to live not in fear or mistrust but to take stock of how I felt emotionally and physically in all things, whether that is around family and friends or dating someone. I evaluate my feelings first and determine the actions that would give me the desired outcome.

An example is when I used to work in a high-stress environment that increased my anxiety and depression from being overly stressed. Did I like the income? Yes, I did, but mentally I was not at my best. I started becoming depressed every time I had to go to work. I did not socialize because I was always tired and exhausted. I felt mentally depleted. I had to make a decision, stay for the money, and suffer mentally, or find another job that gave me less income but afforded me the ability to be less depressed and suffer less anxiety. Was money more important than my wellbeing, or could I still live a comfortable life and be in a better position mentally? These were questions I constantly asked myself when I made a decision that would affect my mental health. Putting myself first, trusting in my feelings and emotions became a requirement in my life.

Once I made these requirements in my life, my path became clearer. I was able to appreciate my decisions more and know that I made the best decisions for myself. When I decided to put myself first, I felt as though I was being selfish and inconsiderate where others were concerned. It made me uncomfortable because I spent so many years putting the needs and desires of everyone around me before my own. I felt I was not good enough to be put first above anyone because of how damaged I still was psychologically. Yes, I still journaled and recorded my thoughts and emotions, but now it took on a different tone, gone was the anger from the abuse that Damien did to me. Now, in its place were unworthiness and insecurities.

My battle was never-ending and I had grown tired of having to fight this internal battle on a daily basis. Why was healing not a one and done thing? Why did I constantly have to need self-reassurance? The world around me continues on as though I wasn't going through constant turmoil. That was when I had an epiphany-the world doesn't stop because of my struggles and pain. It doesn't wait for me to dig myself out of my misery. It doesn't slow down and wait for me because I am tired. I had to be okay with it moving on without me while I sorted my mental state out by myself. I had to learn how to be okay with people living their best lives while I struggled internally and not be jealous of others who were not waiting for me to be okay.

Learning this gave me the encouragement I needed to be selfish about putting myself first because I was obligated to myself and no one else. The life I was living had to be on my terms, not society's. Breaking from the mold that society created was terrifying, I could not depend on other people to fix my insecurities and unworthiness, I had to do that alone. I grew to love my journey, be less dependent on family and friends for reassurance, and find peace being on my healing journey alone.

When I started my journey to heal my mental wounds I thought I only needed to get from point A to point B and call it a day. I never knew I would learn how to love myself, take care of my emotional well-being, and understand why being sexually abused as a child was controlling my life as an adult. I used to think *I survived, so why am I still damaged?* What I learned was that therapy and medication could not heal my moral injuries; the injuries that were done to my conscience due to my sexual trauma. Yes, I was able to get my bipolar disorder, PTSD, nightmares, and anxiety disorder somewhat under control, but that did not mean I did not still suffer nor that they went away altogether. I had to want better and do better for myself, I had to put in the mental work that was needed to get over the ever-present psychological consequences of being a childhood rape victim, one of the biggest consequences being my inability to trust in myself. I needed to break the chain that prevented me from living my best life link by link.

Coming to this realization made me feel more optimistic about my future. It encouraged me to go the extra mile each and every time I had a setback; whether that was having a manic episode that cost me thousands of dollars because buying seven round trip non-refundable tickets all over Europe and Asia sounded like the best freaking idea possible at the time and not going on any of them because they no longer interested me or because I actually forgot the days I had a plan the trip and end up missing all my flights. Coming down from my manic episode, I realized how much money I spent; which was all the money I had in my savings account that was supposed to go towards buying a house. I became angry at myself and fell into a depression from financial loss. This also led to the realization that I had a chronic illness and I needed to take extra steps to prevent this kind of behavior from happening again. Did I have a pity party? Sure did, but I knew that I was still a work in progress and although I had all these obstacles in my path, I still kept in my mind that, I would overcome any and everything because I had goals and dreams to accomplish and nothing would stop me from achieving them.

Reflection Questions:

1. Do I trust my instincts?
2. Where do I place myself in my own life? First, middle or last?
3. Do I rely on other people to make me feel good about myself?
4. Have my insecurities and self-doubt gotten in the way of living life on my terms?
5. What is holding me back from accomplishing my dreams and goals?

CHAPTER 7

Learning to Live Beyond My Sexual Trauma

During the pandemic of 2020, the one where the United States ran out of toilet paper and everything was going awry, you know the one I am talking about. I had a lot of time to do some self-reflecting and dedicate myself to my mental health and wellbeing. The more I focused on myself, the more I began to see that I had not given myself permission to let go of my trauma, meaning I was not letting myself be happy because I felt that my inner child suffered so much that I had to continue suffering as an adult. In order to prove to my inner child that her feelings were not inadequate; in order to prove to her that I did not forget, nor did I want to forget, I had to continue to suffer.

Though I journaled and recorded my feelings on a daily basis to get my anger out, I held on to the pain of my sexual trauma because I did not know how to live without the pain and suffering. After suffering for more than 22 years, I was comfortable being in constant pain mentally, having anxiety attacks on a daily basis, being afraid to sleep at night due to nightmares that plagued me the moment I laid my head to rest, and having extreme bouts of anger, denial, and extreme depression. I felt comfortable in that pain and misery. It was all I knew from the age of seven to the age of twenty-eight. I never considered life without these constant negative feelings and emotions.

It took me quite some time to trust myself and my feelings. I decided to give myself the benefit of the doubt and to prove that I am a trustworthy person, I had to first validate my feelings and trust in myself. For me, trusting in myself meant giving myself permission to stop being weighed down by my trauma and scrutinizing the details surrounding my rape, and letting myself embrace my feelings. By doing this, I began to live a free life without the burden of my traumatic past.

Learning to live without suffering was one of my biggest accomplishments. This accomplishment surpassed receiving my Bachelor's in International Business, my Master's in Political Communication, serving my country for four years in the United States Navy, and living my dream in Japan. Accomplishing these goals while living with fear and suffering, taught me that life can move forward even though such burdens exist. However, life was much better when those negative feelings and emotions were not present. I learned that I can create a life on my terms, a life that is safe, secure, one that I can live without inhibition. My sexual trauma does not have to be the one steering the ship. Validating my feelings and emotions gave me the right to experience and feel whatever emotions I was having and understanding that my sexual trauma was not my fault.

Living beyond my trauma meant I had not let my abuser win by being trapped in my emotions and suffering pain and shame for what I felt during those years. It meant every decision I made after my abuse was one that I wanted to make on my terms. I told myself I can live on my terms as well by laying the blame at the feet of Damien, my abuser. After all, it was he, not I, who was responsible for what I went through.

Reflection Questions:

1. Have I given myself permission to heal from my sexual trauma?
2. What is holding me back from healing from my past trauma?
3. Have I allowed myself to FEEL the emotions associated with my trauma and validate those feelings?
4. Is my sexual trauma in control of how I live my life?
5. Have I allowed myself to place the blame at my abuser's feet?

CHAPTER 8

Accepting My Abuser Was Free and Wouldn't Face Justice

When a child is telling a story, it's never a straight path with a clear beginning, middle, and end. Before they get to the heart of the matter, they have taken you over a bridge, through a tunnel, and between the bushes, to get to the end of the story. Listening to your inner child and consoling her is pretty much the same thing. You have to trust in yourself and that what she is trying to explain will eventually make sense. You have to be patient. You have to be understanding. You have to be willing to listen.

When I decided that I was going to stop fighting against myself and listen to my inner child, I felt emotions so overwhelming that I cried for days. I yelled, I screamed, and I said all the "F yous" for every time Damien ever abused me, for every hurt, every degrading thing I've ever been through and felt in my life, for all the emotional and physical trauma I had ever endured. I said, a big "F you" to Damien and the universe. During my healing process, I realized the universe was not at fault. Damien took advantage of me. He stole from me. He took what was not his to take and no one else is to be blamed but him. So I placed the blame at his feet. I learned that in order to heal, I have to accept the past and embrace my feelings without judging myself. No, I could not call myself negative names, because I was taken advantage of as a child by an adult who should have known better but chose to prey on an innocent child.

I remember when I finally accepted that I was a victim of child rape and that my abuser still walked freely without being held accountable, I was so frustrated to know that he was living his best life, it was a constant trigger for me knowing Damien could be doing this to some other girls and feeling as though I was responsible because I never spoke out against him. I felt I was allowing other children to be caught up in the same mess that I was caught up in as a child. I learned that I have an obligation to no one but myself. Yes, being a good Samaritan is morally preferred. However, you are only obligated to yourself. If I was unable to carry on knowing my abuser was free, then he was winning all over again. I had to live knowing that this predator was walking the Earth, not being held accountable and living life as if he did not ruin mine.

I had to find a way to live my life and learn how to minimize my triggers; whether that was reading about pedophiles in the news, or watching the interactions between a female child and her father interact-hugging, playing, etc. I had, control my emotions, and not have my emotions controlling me. In order to learn what my triggers were, I had to dig deep. I had to physically and mentally take notes and journalize each event which led to me having an anxiety attack, or an angry outburst, or emotionally shutting down as this was how I reacted when I was triggered. I had to ask myself what were some of the reasons why I was constantly in a state of anxiety. Was it the fact that he wasn't held responsible? Yes. Was it the fact that he had children? Yes. Or that I blamed everyone around me for my trauma? Irrationally, yes. Rationally I know that I should not blame anyone else but the man who abused me. I had to figure out this myriad of complex factors and find a way to live my life, knowing that Damien was free.

I had to stop judging myself and stop judging my feelings. In order to do so, I accepted that I had a right to be hurt. I had a right to be angry, and want justice for the actions of this man. I had to accept my feelings and emotions without judging myself in the process.

Reflection Questions:

1. How do I feel knowing my abuser is walking free?
2. What would I say to someone who told me they were a victim of rape?
3. Am I judging myself for being a victim of rape?
4. Do I know what my triggers are?
5. What do I do when I am triggered?

CHAPTER 9

Living In My Window

In my early 20s, I suffered from extreme mood swings, mania, and depression, otherwise referred to as bipolar one disorder. My moods were either extremely high or extremely low, and I could not find a middle ground of stability. Medications were either making me numb to the world or had me in a constant daze. Clarity was never seen during those times, and as a survivor, clarity is one thing that I sought the most. In order to assist in the healing process, I learned that to stabilize my emotions on a daily basis, I had to understand my window of tolerance and what I could do in situations that disrupted my window of tolerance.

By jotting down my daily emotional state and the events surrounding them, I was able to create a clear and concise map of my emotional threshold. In doing so, I was able to pinpoint my level of tolerance and how to control my emotions when it was disrupted. The first thing I had to figure out was whether I was in a state of hyper-arousal. Was I hypervigilant about my surroundings? Were my thoughts racing? Am I experiencing symptoms of anxiety? I had to determine if my fight or flight response was triggered. If I checked all these boxes in my head, I knew I was in a hyper-arousal frame of mind. On the other hand, if I was experiencing feelings of emotional numbness, not having a positive or negative emotional response to a situation, feelings of paralysis, or my brain shutting down to protect itself. In some cases, this feels like I am physically present but nobody is home in my brain, I know I was experiencing hypo-arousal.

I did my research online and spoke to my therapist about how to better understand what I needed to look out for in regards to my window of tolerance. I also had to do an internal search for behaviors that I exhibit when I am approaching that threshold. What I found was by documenting my emotional threshold, I am able to recognize my symptoms of mania and depression along with my daily emotional tolerance level. For instance, not sleeping for 72 hours would be the first red flag of an oncoming manic episode. Another example is when I felt that I didn't need my medication and stopped taking it because I was on top of the world. Nothing anyone said or did would bring down my mood. These were warning signs for me.

When the depression hit, I would no longer wish to get out of bed. I would not shower or brush my teeth or my hair because it was not on my to-do list in fact nothing was on my to-do list. When I started writing down the occurrences that took place before a manic episode or a depressive episode, I started seeing patterns in my behaviors. These patterns were what I like to call my *yellow lights* or *caution ahead: things are about to get real* signs. Now that I know what signs to watch for when it comes to my level of tolerance, I need to learn the techniques that will help me to stay in my threshold or return to my threshold when I experience either hyper-arousal and hypo-arousal. Once I realized I was outside of my window of tolerance, implementing these techniques repeatedly throughout my day helped me build resilience against unwanted negative emotions and gave me the opportunity to be level headed in order to make decisions with rational thought.

Another method is the five senses technique which utilizes the five senses: hearing, sight, smell, touch, and taste. In a moment of feeling out of control, you focus on what you hear around you, what you immediately see, and what you immediately feel or what you taste in your mouth at that moment. I remember using this technique while in a shopping mall. Someone passed me, and he had on the same cologne that my abuser used. This immediately threw me back into a flashback. I was so fearful and so unsure of my predicament that I ended up having an anxiety attack. I had to talk myself down from this attack, as I wasn't around friends, family or my therapist. To do this, I focused on my five senses. What could I see? The man walking past in the blue shirt with the cargo pants. He's holding his wife's hand, and she's holding her daughter's hand. They look like a happy family. This, in turn, made me happy. I could hear the rustle and bustle of shoes on concrete and kids screaming, as they played tag with each other. I could feel the sun on my skin, the warm tingly feeling that let me know that I was okay and safe. I had to use my five senses in order to talk myself down from having a breakdown in the middle of the mall. Using a simple technique that I can implement within seconds of experiencing flashbacks or anxiety attacks, I am able to better control my emotional tolerance and unexpected situations that arise that remind me of my abuse.

Being able to control situations that negatively affect you, helps create positive changes in your healing journey. It allows you to feel in control of your surroundings and makes you trust in your ability to maintain control of your emotions and feelings when triggered. For survivors, controlling your triggers is one of the hardest and most rewarding accomplishments you can achieve in your healing journey. Being able to believe in yourself and your abilities to overcome negative emotions and feelings creates a sense of stability in one's life.

In this chapter you will discover the Trigger Tracker and The window of Tolerance Activity sheet which I use to identify my triggers and recognize when I am outside my window of tolerance.

Trigger Tracker

How Not To Use This Activity Sheet

The activity sheet provided is an educational resource and should not be considered a replacement for professional mental health services and treatment. If you are keenly aware of situations, emotions, and experiences that are triggering for you, this activity sheet may not likely be a beneficial practice. This activity sheet was not created to identify triggers in order to avoid those said triggers.

The educational resources available in this book were created for people who are not consciously aware of situations, encounters, or responses, etc., that are triggering to them and who have the necessary support to begin examining these topics. Adjacent to mental health services and treatment plans, the activity sheets provided may help identify triggers to engage them, recondition them, and heal.

MONIQUE PETERKIN

Trigger Tracker

Date & Time: _____

Emotion(s) that I am feeling.

- _____
- _____
- _____
- _____
- _____
- _____

Six things that happen today.

_____

What triggered my emotions today?

_____

IT WAS HIM, NOT ME

WINDOW OF TOLERANCE AWARENESS WORKSHEET

Identify, recognize the symptoms you experience and build awareness

HYPERAROUSAL

For HYPERAROUSAL, check all the symptoms you experience and enter the level of severity from 1 to 5 (one is the least severe and five is extreme and paralyzing):
- Abnormal state of increased responsiveness
- Feeling anxious, angry and out of control
- You may experience wanting to fight or run away

○ ___ Anxiety	○ ___ Addictions
○ ___ Impulsivity	○ ___ Over-Eating
○ ___ Intense Reactions	○ ___ Obsessive Thoughts/Behaviour
○ ___ Lack of Emotional Safety	○ ___ Emotional Outbursts
○ ___ Hyper-Vigilance	○ ___ Chaotic Responses
○ ___ Intrusive Imagery	○ ___ Defensiveness
○ ___ Tension	○ ___ Racing Thoughts
○ ___ Shaking	○ ___ Anger/Rage
○ ___ Rigidity	○ ___ Physical and Emotional Aggression
○ ___ _____	○ ___ _____
○ ___ _____	○ ___ _____

HYPOAROUSAL

For HYPOAROUSAL, check all the symptoms you experience and enter the level of severity from 1 to 5 (one is the least severe and five is extreme and paralyzing):
- Abnormal state of decreased responsiveness
- Feeling emotional numbness, exhaustion, and depression
- You may experience your body shutting down or freeze

○ ___ The feeling of being disconnected	○ ___ Decreased Reactions
○ ___ No Display of Emotions	○ ___ Shame/Embarrassment
○ ___ Auto-Pilot Responses	○ ___ Depression
○ ___ Memory Loss	○ ___ Difficulty Engaging Coping Resources
○ ___ Feign Death Response	○ ___ Low Levels of Energy
○ ___ Numbness	○ ___ Can't Defend Oneself
○ ___ Disabled Cognitive Processing	○ ___ Shutdown
○ ___ Reduced Physical Movement	○ ___ Can't Say No
○ ___ _____	○ ___ _____
○ ___ _____	○ ___ _____

© 2020 BANANA TREE LOG
www.bananatreelog.com

Reflection Questions:

1. How can I tell when I am no longer in control of my emotions?
2. What negative emotions can I identify when I am hyper-aroused/ hypo-aroused?
3. What do I do if I am experiencing emotion disruptions? (anxiety/panic attacks, anger, frustration etc.]
4. How often am I triggered?
5. Am I able to achieve emotional stability after a trigger?

CHAPTER 10

My Nights Were Not My Own; They Were For My Demons

I never used to consider nighttime as a time to recharge, rest, and to heal my body after a day of physical activities and mental challenges. I stayed up as long as physically possible, the longest being 72 hours. I was afraid to sleep, for many years I thought that my nights were not my own; they were for my demons. When someone mentioned sleep, I would immediately go into a silent anxiety attack, thinking about my demons reaching out, grabbing me, and dragging me down into an abyss. I did not associate nighttime with any positive emotions. Therefore, I tried to avoid it at all costs. But the sun will always shine, and night will always come. I learned that sleep deprivation cannot be cured with seven cups of coffee with triple shots of espresso, in a four-hour time span. In fact, I can guarantee you, you will puke your guts out and feel horrible in the process, all while still being sleep deprived. I feared sleeping because it brought me back to my childhood. I thought sleep deprivation was the only thing that could prevent that. Boy, was I wrong.

My discovery of weighted blankets was like discovering that bread can be sliced: the best thing ever. Weighted blankets can be found on any online platform such as Amazon or eBay, as well as local stores selling bedding. When I discovered weighted blankets, I thought this was going to be confinement at its finest—smothering and overwhelming. I did not think that weighted blankets would be a miracle worker. I did not think they were going to help me with my situation of fearing the night and fearing sleep, but I gave it a try because I had nothing to lose.

My reaction to the effect of a weighted blanket astonishment. As a person who does not like to be touched unless I initiate the contact first, I felt safe and secured while under the blanket. As though this blanket knew what I had been through and knew I needed a little more than the average weight on a regular blanket in order to feel protected against my demons and nightmares. It also helped with the anxiety I experienced at night whenever I got into bed. I started looking forward to sleep or just being under the blanket when the world around me made me feel unsure of my place. I was comforted by the weight of the blanket which was a surprise in itself, it was one of my best purchases.

Self-care does not always mean manicures and pedicures, even though those are awesome and do make you feel pretty. Self-care, however, also means taking care of your emotional and physical well-being. When you deprive yourself of sleep or any positive emotional activities that assist with your well-being, you are creating a dangerous situation for yourself. You are self-sabotaging. Why would you not want the best for yourself if you want the best for others? Your emotional well being is as important as your physical well-being. Taking care of yourself is how you are able to continue the good fight. It is also how you are able to make sound decisions, judgments, and feels good about yourself.

For me, taking care of my emotional well being meant I had to find techniques that contributed positively to my emotional state. My mind gets too loud or chaotic and I am unable to quiet my thoughts. I searched for ways that I could quiet my mind while achieving clarity. After reading about meditation and hearing my good friend rave about the silence you have once you hit that plateau of deep meditation, I decided I would try anything to quiet the noise in my head. The first time I tried guided meditation, I scared myself when I reached that deep state of meditation where all things fall away. I did not hear sounds; no laughter or voices. Anything that can be heard in the outside world dropped away. Every inner turmoil, inner discussions, inner dialogue, all stop; everything becomes quiet, leaving you in a blanketed space of bliss and utter silence.

Now, as a person who has never been able to quiet the turmoil in my head and put aside the outside world, I was scared. It was a new level of profound realization that I can create an exclusive space just for me. By simply not participating in society for a few minutes of the day, I was able to recharge my battery from zero percent to 1,000 percent, and I did this by reaching the deep state of meditation in which I chose to become one with my mind. I didn't fight against the current. I did not worry about answering my phone. I did not worry about checking my Instagram nor my Facebook. I simply existed in a moment of time, and the clarity that I gained was unreal.

Another form of self-care I advocate for is having a balanced diet. Don't get me wrong, pizza and wings sound freaking amazing, and add a bottle of beer, and you are set. But what we must not forget is that our body needs nutritious food, water, and vitamins to function optimally, to meet the physical demands of our daily life, and to maintain our emotional well being. When you look good, you feel good; if your body is not getting its most basic needs met, then it is time to think about changing up your routine. I have gone through countless workout programs and countless fad diets to achieve the maximum results in the shortest amount of time. However, as the experts say, a shortcut isn't always the best cut.

I decided to give my body what it needed, balanced nutrition by figuring out the foods I enjoyed eating, and those I could live without eating. I wanted to avoid sending myself into a restrictive diet but also preventing myself from binging on fast food. I had to find food and recipes that I like, which was trial and error, in order to come up with my own personal meal plan that was both tasty and nutritional. The first time that I gave it an honest shot, I felt satisfied and fulfilled. Focusing on your emotional and physical well-being is a part of the healing process that should not be forgotten and should not be put on the back burner. It is important and it is necessary to incorporate it into your healing journey. Your physical and emotional well-being are the two sides of the same coin.

Reflection Questions:

1. What are the ways my sexual trauma affects me physically?
2. What are the shortcuts I take to achieve my physical and work goals?
3. How can I improve my physical health and maintain it?
4. What are my self-care techniques?
5. Has my physical health been affected by my mental health?

CHAPTER 11

This Is My Story I Will Use My Voice

The first time I told someone outside of my therapist that I was abused as a child, I lost all sense of rational thinking. I was angry, frustrated, and felt backed in a corner, and the only way to take back control of the situation was to lash out and hurt any and everyone I came across. That person was my mom. Could I have handled the situation in which I told her about my abuse differently? I'm sure I could have, however at the time, before the journaling and recording of my thoughts, feelings, and emotions, I did not know how to control my reactions when I spoke about my childhood. It took a few years in therapy before I was able to control it. Prior to that, I was not at the place mentally where I could talk about being raped without getting angry and resentful. Emotions are like an unopened bottle of soda. If you constantly shake that bottle and then rip the cap off like it's no big deal, you and anyone within the vicinity are about to get real messy.

The environment in which you disclose personal information, such as sexual abuse can create scenarios that are damaging. You need to prepare to possibly lose some friends and family members when you disclose your sexual trauma. Not everyone is going to be on your side. Not everyone is going to believe you or side with you. They may either dismiss your claims or make you an outcast. Not everyone will stand in your corner when you decide to come forward about your abuse. They may pick the side of your abuser. In fact, some people will call you a liar, a family destroyer for calling out your abuser(s), and even say that you are making the abuse up because you are an unruly person and just want to see others suffer. And then you will be left picking up the pieces because you decided to open up about your trauma.

On the flip side, opening up about your trauma can invite more love, more support than you could possibly imagine. Your family and friends who do not shun you will start to understand why you behave the way you behave and why you say the things that you say. They will start to comprehend that there will be situations that are hard to discuss and hard to handle. They will still support you no matter what, loving you more fiercely without pity. They will let you know that they are grateful you took the time to explain your sexual trauma to them. There are always two sides to a coin; both positive and negative sides can affect how you move forward with your healing process. But once you have an understanding that you will come across people who react negatively to your opening up about your sexual trauma, you will have a better grasp on how to deal with that situation, and how to lessen the impact of those negative emotions that arise in you when you are faced with negative feedback about your experience.

What I learned is that the truth will set you free. In some cases, it lands your abuser(s) behind bars. In other cases, it will at least lessen the burden that you have shouldered for so many years. Best case scenario you will no longer have to shoulder it by yourself. Worst case scenario you learn who the people are who have your back and those who do not. It is such a liberating feeling to be able to speak openly about your trauma, whether that's in a group setting on social media, to your family, or to your friends. Speaking about your trauma relieves that secret that has been eating you up inside, that has made you feel like a failure or someone not meant to be loved, cherished, or validated. All those feelings will eventually cease to exist as you get more comfortable with being open about your trauma to those whom you trust.

There will be moments of clarity, stability, and even moments of emotional disturbance, but you will feel lighter in the end. It will give you peace to know you no longer have to have these secrets plague your every waking moment and dream state. You will no longer feel as though your tongue is tied or that you are going to get in trouble or as though your parents will hate you if you don't keep your trauma all to yourself. Speaking about your trauma will alleviate your stress, in many ways, and make the healing journey that much easier as time passes.

Reflection Questions:

1. If I could tell my story to someone, who would that be??
2. What are my emotional and physical reactions when I think about my sexual trauma?

3. Whom do I trust to share my abuse with?
4. Do I feel the burden surrounding my sexual trauma will be less if I open up about it? Why, or why not?
5. What is the worst that could happen if I open up about my past trauma?

CHAPTER 12

This Is My Body, And I Am In Charge

When I started my healing journey, one of my main priorities was learning how to love my body and embrace my feelings at the moment and thereafter. Throughout this book, I have shared how I embrace my feelings quite frequently. This is because, during traumatic events, we as humans have a tendency to put aside or to neglect our feelings to persevere or protect our mental health. By embracing your feelings, you are given permission to feel without judgment. By changing the negative narrative to one that is more positive, you will be able to change your mindset and how you view yourself. Individuals who have suffered sexual trauma have a difficult time with self-acceptance, self-love, and happiness.

I stopped looking in the mirror because I did not like who was looking back at me. It took me a few years before I started facing my reflections in the mirror and really looked at the person staring back at me. I talked to myself. I asked my reflection questions about what I liked, what I disliked, what I was okay with, and what I wasn't okay with when it came to my best interest. I journaled the feelings I uncovered from the answers. This is how I started unraveling the real me, the real Monique as opposed to the Monique who said yes to everyone, the people-pleaser Monique, the I'll-do-anything-so-long-as-you-will be-my-friend Monique.

I had to learn how to stop hating myself and start loving myself. I had to learn what pleases me and stop doing what only pleased others around me. I had to figure out how to put myself first and foremost. I started using positive reassuring words and phrases daily such as; I cannot blame my body for what was done to it. I can nurture and cherish it, and I can love it as only I can. My feelings are valid to me and how I feel matters. By doing this, I gave myself permission to accept that I was a victim of sexual abuse, but I was not responsible. I had nothing to forgive myself for because it was not my fault. Instead of hating my body and how I felt about myself, I embraced it. I took charge of my physical self and I gave it what it needed to thrive and move forward. I accepted what I could not change and focused my attention on what I could change and control.

As survivors, we often recognize during the healing process that we tend to blame our physical being and our mental state for how we process and understand these traumatic circumstances or events. We also tend to want to neglect our bodies, to avoid the reminder of what we went through. By not actively reconnecting with our bodies and our feelings, we are burying our heads in the sand and pretending it didn't happen. By reconnecting with your body and your feelings, you are increasing your resilience and strength so you can heal and live beyond your trauma.

How can I love somebody else if I cannot love myself? I am averse to this sort of thought process because I feel like yes, I can love other people in my own way, even if I don't love myself. There can be characteristics and personality traits I see in someone I admire and that I grow emotionally attached to, and I love them because of what they represent and the image that they portray.

Not loving yourself doesn't mean that you don't have room to love other people. However, it does hinder how you think others view you. Therefore, your trust will not be 100% because you will wonder how other people love you if you do not love yourself, this will become the way I thought, and it was ingrained in me. I thought people were lying when they said they love me because I did not love myself and that means others could love me because I did not accept myself for who I was.

You may have not delved deeply enough into understanding your self-worth to find the self-respect and internal happiness to decide to love yourself because of what you endure at the hands of your abuser(s). One of the best parts of reconnecting with your body and feelings is learning the different aspects of yourself and figuring out what your moral and ethical values are.

Reflection Questions:

1. Do I like the person in the mirror who is looking back at me?
2. Do I love myself?
3. Do I love the body I am in?
4. What does self-acceptance mean to me?
5. Am I worthy of self-love?

CHAPTER 13

The Manipulated Becomes the Manipulator

Men are not the only ones who sexually manipulate women to feel in control. Women do this too. I did not have sex because it gave me orgasms. In fact, I did not even believe women could have orgasms. I thought that it was strictly a male thing. I had sex because the only interaction I knew how to have with a male partner was with my body. I did not know anything about relationships; therefore, I kept on giving my body, often hurting myself in the process. I kept my interactions with men strictly sexual. It was a way I could control a person with their consent. I was taking charge of what giving my body meant, oftentimes putting myself in dangerous situations. The universe has been on my side because nothing has happened, and I am eternally grateful. Using sex to manipulate others so you feel in control of yourself does not cure your feelings. I learned that I had to change the narrative of how I viewed sex to enjoy it without needing to manipulate my lovers or needing to feel like proving to myself and to my abusers that I have gotten over my trauma.

The first time I had sex without feeling the need to manipulate my lover, I felt vulnerable and anxious. I was so used to having my armor in place and dictating the details of how the encounter would go that I forgot I was supposed to be enjoying it. I learned that using my body as a weapon was hurting not just myself, but putting myself and my partners at risk. Learning what I like and dislike helped me to reclaim my sexual self and helped me in deciding which sexual acts were for me and which were to prove a point to myself that sex does not have to include manipulation, it does not have to be an obligation. I had to prove to myself that I can have sex and enjoy it because I want to and not because I was groomed for it.

One of the things that I have experienced in my adult life is an overactive sex drive. For me that came in the form of having excessive thoughts about sexual fantasies. My urges or behaviors that caused me distress and anxiety became difficult to control. It impacted my work and started to be noticeable to my friends. I learned that I experienced an overactive sex drive due to my sexual trauma as a child. I did not like when guys initiate sex with me; I had to be the one to initiate it or it would be a turn off for me.

Learning to allow my partner to take the lead was difficult. I had to respect that he had needs too and I did not need to control every aspect of intercourse. Changing how I viewed sex took time and patience. I had to learn how to be intimate with a person. I had to recognize what areas of my body and sexual positions were off-limits due to them being triggers for me. I began to enjoy foreplay and letting my partner take the lead. Having a clear understanding of the limits you are not willing to cross sexually will help your partner to pleasure you better without triggering you. I had to trust in myself and trust in another human being to not cross the boundaries I set. This was also a healing moment for me as I started to extend my trust outwards and let someone in. Letting my guard down meant I was giving someone the power to hurt me but trusting them not to. Once that trust was built, I began to slowly extend that trust to my immediate family, close friends, and sexual partner.

Reflection Questions:

1. Do I use sex as a way to feel in control?
2. Do I use sex to manipulate my partner?
3. Do I have a healthy understanding of sexual intimacy?
4. Am I able to let my partner take the lead or do I have to be the one always in control?
5. Do I feel obligated to have sexual intimacy with my partner?

CHAPTER 14

Taking back my happiness

B ack in 2017, I recall saying to my therapist, "You know I've actually never been happy. I can't recall a time in my life in which I was happy. I've smiled about what people have said, I've laughed about things I have found funny or hysterical, but I can never truly remember a time in my life that I have been truly happy."

I didn't know what it felt like to be happy. I was a stranger to that emotion even in my accomplishments, my travel adventures, and my electronic toys. They never brought me happiness. With the way I felt about my sexual trauma, I could not see myself being happy in the future, and I wanted to change that. I would stand and look at families and friends and see them gush and compliment each other and say how happy they were and how amazing their life is. Don't get me wrong, I understand that not everyone's life is perfect, and people tend to put up a front to please and show off. Even with that knowledge, I've never really experienced that emotion and I was envious of those who did.

Through my journey to reclaiming my power and learning to live beyond childhood sexual trauma, I learned that I am in control of my happiness; no one else can control it. I can decide to stay in misery, or I can work towards healing myself and embracing my feelings and emotions by learning to be happy doing what I love to do on my own terms. If you're in a job that makes you unhappy and weighs you down, you may need to leave for the sake of your peace and mental health. You will feel a measurable change in your mood and mental health once you remove yourself from the environment that is causing you distress. Now that's easier said than done. I do understand that, but at the same time, if you are able to contribute anything towards your happiness, it is making the decision to take yourself out of the situation that is making you unhappy. I found that what truly made me happy was spending time with myself. I absolutely enjoyed my alone time. I also enjoy just sitting and not having to be a part of the conversation, not having to give my input, and not having to be included in the conversation. I was quite okay with just sitting and watching the interactions of people that I care about and admire.

I also found out I had a passion for education. I am the type of person who loves to learn new things. I love to learn new ways to communicate with people. I had a desire to better understand my bipolar disorder, anger, post-traumatic stress disorder (PTSD), anxiety attacks, and nightmares because I was experiencing them. I was fascinated by these things, and I found I was truly happy when I was researching and learning new information and strategies to help me. I was happy when I was allowing myself to heal.

Now, this is not to say that this won't change in the next several weeks, months, or years, but at this point in my life, I can truly say I have found happiness within myself by acknowledging and accepting I was a victim of childhood rape, taking back my power from my abuser, exploring my mental illness, exploring the world, traveling, hiking, reading books, and creating healthy techniques that may help the next person who has experienced trauma similar to mine. I was done trying to fit into society's view of what should make me happy. I was done living my life based on somebody else's expectations. The easiest way to break away from that restraint was literally to look inside myself and realize that I'm not going to let somebody else control my emotions or how I live my life. I am going to forge my own path. I am discovering who I am as a person, and that person is the bomb dot com! I know that I am amazing, adventurous, articulate, and forgiving. I am a person who loves to please other people, but I still set my boundaries so I can please other people and still be happy with myself. This is what I had to uncover all on my own.

No amount of medication or therapy was able to teach me how to trust in me, validate my feelings, how to be happy. I have to figure out my own feelings, my own intuition, and my own instincts. I have to embrace myself and be okay with who I am as a person and what I uncover about myself as time went by. Deciding if there are things that make me happy was not up to anyone but myself. I had to make the decisions on what I deemed acceptable and was in my best interest. I had to figure out and accept that I am more than my sexual trauma.

The decision to be happy and find contentment is no one else's but my own. People who rely on others to make them happy and content oftentimes find themselves being resentful when their expectations are not met by someone else. They may find that what makes other people happy doesn't necessarily make them happy. Sometimes we are afraid to step out of our comfort zone and find what makes us happy because we have no clue where to begin. We often do not want to challenge the norm out of fear of being shunned by those we consider family and friends.

I became the person who challenges the norm, to step outside my comfort zone, to create my own path to healing and success. I am no longer the woman who sees herself as damaged and unworthy. I am a woman who has battle scars. I am a woman who is worthy of love and happiness and all things good. This is my journey to healing the psychological wounds of childhood rape. This is my journey of reclaiming my power which my abuser stole from me. This is me living beyond my sexual trauma. I stopped struggling against my emotions and embraced them; I healed from them and believed in myself because I needed to in order to be happy, find inner peace and acceptance were vital to my happy state of mind. And happiness is just that, a state of mind. It does not necessarily last in the sense I will never feel any negative emotions again, but it is knowing that I have made choices and done everything in my power to fulfil my desires, and whatever obligation I have to myself and be content about what I have accomplished. It is knowing that the decisions I have made will leave a positive impact on my life and others. Once I was able to reach that level of contentment with those decisions I was able to unlock true success and happiness, in both my personal and professional life.

That was when I realized that my search for happiness meant I had to be content with every decision I made and stay true to them. Staying true to myself was the key to my healing journey.

Reflection Question:

1. Am I happy with how my life is currently going?
2. Is my environment beneficial to my mental and physical health?
3. Do I rely on others to make me happy?
4. What does contentment mean to me?
5. Am I content with the decisions I have made in my life?

Conclusion

This book is about living beyond your trauma; it is about finding out what your triggers are and using coping mechanisms to live with the fact that your abuser or abusers are still out there, still free to roam, not being charged for what they did to you. It is about finding that inner peace, located deep within yourself and understanding that yes this happened to you. And you know you were a victim at one point, but now you are a survivor. You have found the tools to use in your daily life that can elevate you from being a victim and turn you into a survivor and a victor. You can take control of your emotions and your feelings, restoring your self-worth and yourself image and moving away from self-hatred and self-loathing. These are unique to you and only you.

There's not a prototype out there that's going to fit every person. The only way you can find what is uniquely yours is by looking into yourself and discovering who you are.

After my trauma, it took me a long time' and it took some work and it was frustrating. It's emotionally draining, but at the same time, the outcome of being happy is well worth the journey. It's worth using these strategies and coping mechanisms to find out who you are, what your triggers are, how you can alleviate these triggers and how to start living your life beyond trauma.

You can learn to give your best self while still being cautious and remembering who you are as a person and knowing you still need your space to recharge, especially if you're antisocial or if you are an introvert.

At the end of day, everyone still needs to recharge, and find that threshold, in other words your window of tolerance. Understanding your body and your mind will lead you to a happier place in a more content environment. It will lead you to live a future on your terms, and that it is worth having. Trauma does not define us as individuals. What we do and how we react to that trauma is what defines us, and at the end of the day, seeking out happiness beyond trauma will show our perseverance, our never ending resilience as a person. And that's an admirable quality that each of us possess even if it may take you a little bit longer than others to get there. This is your journey— take it for you. You are the super hero in your story.

You owe it to your future self to invest in you. The work companion provided in this book was created to help learn how you can reclaim your sense of self and power and to live the life you dreamt of living without being weighed down by your traumatic past.

This book likely brings back memories we all wish to leave in the past, but have they really been left in the past? Have your past actions and emotions as an adult speak of someone who has survived sexual trauma or has it been those of a victim still being burdened by what was done to her? You will find clarity as you go through each chapter of this book and understand and trust in your feelings and the process as time goes by. This is your journey—make it a kick ass one and embrace the possibilities of living beyond your trauma.

MONIQUE PETERKIN

Date: _____

Journal Entry

How has my thoughts and emotions affected me today?

IT WAS HIM, NOT ME

Date: _____

Journal Entry

How has my thoughts and emotions affected me today?

_____
_____
_____
_____
_____
_____
_____
_____
_____
_____
_____
_____
_____
_____
_____
_____
_____
_____
_____
_____

MONIQUE PETERKIN

Date: _____

Journal Entry

How has my thoughts and emotions affected me today?

_____
_____
_____
_____
_____
_____
_____
_____
_____
_____
_____
_____
_____
_____
_____
_____
_____
_____
_____
_____

IT WAS HIM, NOT ME

Date: _____

Journal Entry

How has my thoughts and emotions affected me today?

_____
_____
_____
_____
_____
_____
_____
_____
_____
_____
_____
_____
_____
_____
_____
_____
_____
_____
_____

Date: _____

Journal Entry

How has my thoughts and emotions affected me today?

_____
_____
_____
_____
_____
_____
_____
_____
_____
_____
_____
_____
_____
_____
_____
_____
_____
_____

IT WAS HIM, NOT ME

Date: _____

Journal Entry

How has my thoughts and emotions affected me today?

MONIQUE PETERKIN

Date: _____

Journal Entry

How has my thoughts and emotions affected me today?

About the Author

Monique Nastasia Peterkin is an aspiring author who has dedicated her life to helping those who have experienced sexual trauma by taking them through a journey of healing to enable them to reclaim their power and take control of their lives again. This is the same journey she passed through victoriously as a survivor of childhood sexual trauma.

Monique attained a bachelor's degree in International Business after which she pursued her Master's in Political Communication. She is currently pursuing a Ph.D. in Trauma Psychology which enables her to assist trauma victims more professionally. As an honourable discharged navy veteran, she is a woman of integrity who advocates for justice for the offended. She is a bold writer who does not shy away from topics that everyone is afraid to talk about. Drawing inspiration from her stories, Monique uses her books as a platform to speak up about issues plaguing society at the moment with her views that are honest and straight from the heart.

Connect with Monique
If you would like to learn more please visit www.moniquepeterkin.com
You can also find her online via your favorite social media platform via the links below.
https://www.facebook.com/Author.MoniquePeterkin
https://twitter.com/Themoniquepete1
https://www.instagram.com/the.moniquepeterkin/

www.ingramcontent.com/pod-product-compliance
Lightning Source LLC
Chambersburg PA
CBHW042342150426
43194CB00028B/10